Under the Canvas

&

Over the MOON

CAMPING JOURNAL

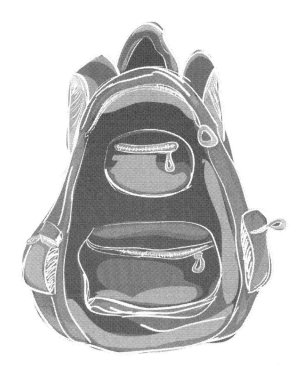

I would rather own little
And see the world
Than own the world
And see little of it.

- A. Sattler

Campground: _____   **Dates:** _____

We Stayed At Site#: _____   Other Sites We Liked: _____

Location: _____

Weather:

Overall, This Campground Was:

☐ Amazing   ☐ Great   ☐ Fun   ☐ Okay

We camped with:

_____

_____

_____

Our favorite thing to do at this campground was:

_____

_____

_____

One thing we'll always remember about this trip was:

_____

_____

_____

If we visited here again, we would be sure to:

_____

_____

Favorite Memories

_____

_____

_____

_____

_____

Favorite Food: (Best camping recipe, favorite ice cream shop, etc.)

_____
_____
_____
_____
_____
_____
_____
_____

Notes:

_____
_____
_____
_____
_____
_____
_____
_____

Favorite Photo:

Campground: _____   Dates: _____

We Stayed At Site#: _____   Other Sites We Liked: _____

Location: _____

Weather: ☀️ ☁️ 🌧️ 🌨️

Overall, This Campground Was:

☐ Amazing   ☐ Great   ☐ Fun   ☐ Okay

We camped with:

_____
_____
_____

Our favorite thing to do at this campground was:

_____
_____
_____

One thing we'll always remember about this trip was:

_____
_____
_____

If we visited here again, we would be sure to:

_____
_____

Favorite Memories

_____
_____
_____
_____

Favorite Food: (Best camping recipe, favorite ice cream shop, etc.)

_____

_____

_____

_____

_____

_____

_____

_____

Notes:

_____

_____

_____

_____

_____

_____

_____

_____

Favorite Photo:

Campground: _____   **Dates:** _____

We Stayed At Site#: _____   Other Sites We Liked: _____

Location: _____

Weather: ☀ ☁ 🌧 🌨

Overall, This Campground Was:
☐ Amazing   ☐ Great   ☐ Fun   ☐ Okay

We camped with:
_____
_____
_____

Our favorite thing to do at this campground was:
_____
_____
_____

One thing we'll always remember about this trip was:
_____
_____
_____

If we visited here again, we would be sure to:
_____
_____

Favorite Memories
_____
_____
_____
_____
_____

Favorite Food: (Best camping recipe, favorite ice cream shop, etc.)

_____
_____
_____
_____
_____
_____
_____

Notes:

_____
_____
_____
_____
_____
_____
_____
_____

Favorite Photo:

Campground: _____ **Dates:** _____

We Stayed At Site#: _____ Other Sites We Liked: _____

Location: _____

Weather: ☀ ☁ 🌧 🌨

Overall, This Campground Was:

☐ Amazing ☐ Great ☐ Fun ☐ Okay

We camped with:

_____

_____

_____

Our favorite thing to do at this campground was:

_____

_____

_____

One thing we'll always remember about this trip was:

_____

_____

_____

If we visited here again, we would be sure to:

_____

_____

Favorite Memories

_____

_____

_____

_____

_____

Favorite Food: (Best camping recipe, favorite ice cream shop, etc.)

_____

_____

_____

_____

_____

_____

_____

_____

Notes:

_____

_____

_____

_____

_____

_____

_____

_____

Favorite Photo:

Campground: _____   **Dates:** _____

We Stayed At Site#: _____   Other Sites We Liked: _____

Location: _____

Weather: ☀ ☁ 🌧 🌨

Overall, This Campground Was:

☐ Amazing   ☐ Great   ☐ Fun   ☐ Okay

We camped with:

_____
_____
_____

Our favorite thing to do at this campground was:

_____
_____
_____

One thing we'll always remember about this trip was:

_____
_____
_____

If we visited here again, we would be sure to:

_____
_____

Favorite Memories

_____
_____
_____
_____
_____

Favorite Food: (Best camping recipe, favorite ice cream shop, etc.)

_____

_____

_____

_____

_____

_____

_____

_____

Notes:

_____

_____

_____

_____

_____

_____

_____

_____

Favorite Photo:

Campground: _____   **Dates:** _____

We Stayed At Site#: _____   Other Sites We Liked: _____

Location: _____

Weather:

Overall, This Campground Was:
☐ Amazing   ☐ Great   ☐ Fun   ☐ Okay

We camped with:
_____
_____
_____

Our favorite thing to do at this campground was:
_____
_____
_____

One thing we'll always remember about this trip was:
_____
_____
_____

If we visited here again, we would be sure to:
_____
_____

Favorite Memories
_____
_____
_____
_____
_____

Favorite Food: (Best camping recipe, favorite ice cream shop, etc.)

_____
_____
_____
_____
_____
_____
_____
_____

Notes:

_____
_____
_____
_____
_____
_____
_____

Favorite Photo:

Campground: _____   Dates: _____

We Stayed At Site#: _____   Other Sites We Liked: _____

Location: _____

Weather:

Overall, This Campground Was:

☐ Amazing   ☐ Great   ☐ Fun   ☐ Okay

We camped with:

_____

_____

_____

Our favorite thing to do at this campground was:

_____

_____

_____

One thing we'll always remember about this trip was:

_____

_____

_____

If we visited here again, we would be sure to:

_____

_____

Favorite Memories

_____

_____

_____

_____

_____

Favorite Food: (Best camping recipe, favorite ice cream shop, etc.)

_____
_____
_____
_____
_____
_____
_____
_____

Notes:

_____
_____
_____
_____
_____
_____
_____
_____

Favorite Photo:

Campground: _____   **Dates:** _____

We Stayed At Site#: _____   Other Sites We Liked: _____

Location: _____

Weather: ☀ ☁ 🌧 🌨

Overall, This Campground Was:

☐ Amazing   ☐ Great   ☐ Fun   ☐ Okay

We camped with:

_____

_____

_____

Our favorite thing to do at this campground was:

_____

_____

_____

One thing we'll always remember about this trip was:

_____

_____

_____

If we visited here again, we would be sure to:

_____

_____

Favorite Memories

_____

_____

_____

_____

_____

Favorite Food: (Best camping recipe, favorite ice cream shop, etc.)

_____

_____

_____

_____

_____

_____

_____

Notes:

_____

_____

_____

_____

_____

_____

_____

_____

Favorite Photo:

Campground: Dates:

We Stayed At Site#: _____   Other Sites We Liked: _____

Location: _____

Weather: **Overall, This Campground Was:**

☐ Amazing   ☐ Great   ☐ Fun   ☐ Okay

We camped with:

_____
_____
_____

Our favorite thing to do at this campground was:

_____
_____
_____

One thing we'll always remember about this trip was:

_____
_____
_____

If we visited here again, we would be sure to:

_____
_____

Favorite Memories

_____
_____
_____
_____
_____

Favorite Food: (Best camping recipe, favorite ice cream shop, etc.)

_____
_____
_____
_____
_____
_____
_____

Notes:

_____
_____
_____
_____
_____
_____
_____

Favorite Photo:

Campground: Dates:

We Stayed At Site#: _____   Other Sites We Liked: _____

Location: _____

Weather:

Overall, This Campground Was:

☐ Amazing   ☐ Great   ☐ Fun   ☐ Okay

We camped with:

_____
_____
_____

Our favorite thing to do at this campground was:

_____
_____
_____

One thing we'll always remember about this trip was:

_____
_____
_____

If we visited here again, we would be sure to:

_____
_____

Favorite Memories

_____
_____
_____
_____

Favorite Food: (Best camping recipe, favorite ice cream shop, etc.)

_____

_____

_____

_____

_____

_____

_____

Notes:

_____

_____

_____

_____

_____

_____

_____

Favorite Photo:

Campground: Dates:

We Stayed At Site#: _____   Other Sites We Liked: _____

Location: _____

Weather:

Overall, This Campground Was:

☐ Amazing   ☐ Great   ☐ Fun   ☐ Okay

We camped with:

_____
_____
_____

Our favorite thing to do at this campground was:

_____
_____
_____

One thing we'll always remember about this trip was:

_____
_____
_____

If we visited here again, we would be sure to:

_____
_____

Favorite Memories

_____
_____
_____
_____
_____

Favorite Food: (Best camping recipe, favorite ice cream shop, etc.)

_____

_____

_____

_____

_____

_____

_____

_____

Notes:

_____

_____

_____

_____

_____

_____

_____

_____

_____

Favorite Photo:

Campground: _____ Dates: _____

We Stayed At Site#: _____ Other Sites We Liked: _____

Location: _____

Weather:

Overall, This Campground Was:

☐ Amazing ☐ Great ☐ Fun ☐ Okay

We camped with:

_____
_____
_____

Our favorite thing to do at this campground was:

_____
_____
_____

One thing we'll always remember about this trip was:

_____
_____
_____

If we visited here again, we would be sure to:

_____
_____

Favorite Memories

_____
_____
_____
_____
_____

Favorite Food: (Best camping recipe, favorite ice cream shop, etc.)

_____
_____
_____
_____
_____
_____
_____

Notes:

_____
_____
_____
_____
_____
_____
_____

Favorite Photo:

Campground: _____   Dates: _____

We Stayed At Site#: _____   Other Sites We Liked: _____

Location: _____

Weather: ☀ ☁ 🌧 🌨

┌───┐
│ Overall, This Campground Was: │
│ ☐ Amazing   ☐ Great   ☐ Fun   ☐ Okay   │
└───┘

We camped with:

_____
_____
_____

Our favorite thing to do at this campground was:

_____
_____
_____

One thing we'll always remember about this trip was:

_____
_____
_____

If we visited here again, we would be sure to:

_____
_____

Favorite Memories

_____
_____
_____
_____

Favorite Food: (Best camping recipe, favorite ice cream shop, etc.)

_____
_____
_____
_____
_____
_____
_____

Notes:

_____
_____
_____
_____
_____
_____
_____
_____

Favorite Photo:

Campground:	Dates:

We Stayed At Site#: _____   Other Sites We Liked: _____

Location: _____

Weather: ☀ ☁ 🌧 🌨

┌───┐
│ Overall, This Campground Was: │
│ ☐ Amazing   ☐ Great   ☐ Fun   ☐ Okay │
└───┘

We camped with:

_____
_____
_____

Our favorite thing to do at this campground was:

_____
_____
_____

One thing we'll always remember about this trip was:

_____
_____
_____

If we visited here again, we would be sure to:

_____
_____

Favorite Memories

_____
_____
_____
_____
_____

Favorite Food: (Best camping recipe, favorite ice cream shop, etc.)

_____
_____
_____
_____
_____
_____
_____
_____

Notes:

_____
_____
_____
_____
_____
_____
_____
_____

Favorite Photo:

Campground: Dates:

We Stayed At Site#: _____   Other Sites We Liked: _____

Location: _____

Weather: Overall, This Campground Was:

☐ Amazing   ☐ Great   ☐ Fun   ☐ Okay

We camped with:

_____
_____
_____

Our favorite thing to do at this campground was:

_____
_____
_____

One thing we'll always remember about this trip was:

_____
_____
_____

If we visited here again, we would be sure to:

_____
_____

Favorite Memories

_____
_____
_____
_____
_____

Favorite Food: (Best camping recipe, favorite ice cream shop, etc.)

_____
_____
_____
_____
_____
_____
_____
_____

Notes:

_____
_____
_____
_____
_____
_____
_____
_____

Favorite Photo:

Campground: _____   **Dates:** _____

We Stayed At Site#: _____   Other Sites We Liked: _____

Location: _____

Weather: ☀   ☁   🌧   🌨

Overall, This Campground Was:

☐ Amazing   ☐ Great   ☐ Fun   ☐ Okay

We camped with:

_____
_____
_____

Our favorite thing to do at this campground was:

_____
_____
_____

One thing we'll always remember about this trip was:

_____
_____
_____

If we visited here again, we would be sure to:

_____
_____

Favorite Memories

_____
_____
_____
_____
_____

Favorite Food: (Best camping recipe, favorite ice cream shop, etc.)

_____
_____
_____
_____
_____
_____
_____

Notes:

_____
_____
_____
_____
_____
_____
_____

Favorite Photo:

Campground: _____ Dates: _____

We Stayed At Site#: _____ Other Sites We Liked: _____

Location: _____

Weather: ☀ ☁ ⛈ ❄

Overall, This Campground Was:

☐ Amazing   ☐ Great   ☐ Fun   ☐ Okay

We camped with:

_____
_____
_____

Our favorite thing to do at this campground was:

_____
_____
_____

One thing we'll always remember about this trip was:

_____
_____
_____

If we visited here again, we would be sure to:

_____
_____

Favorite Memories

_____
_____
_____
_____
_____

Favorite Food: (Best camping recipe, favorite ice cream shop, etc.)

_____
_____
_____
_____
_____
_____
_____
_____

Notes:

_____
_____
_____
_____
_____
_____
_____
_____

Favorite Photo:

Campground: _____ **Dates:** _____

We Stayed At Site#: _____ Other Sites We Liked: _____

Location: _____

Weather:

Overall, This Campground Was:

☐ Amazing   ☐ Great   ☐ Fun   ☐ Okay

We camped with:

_____

_____

_____

Our favorite thing to do at this campground was:

_____

_____

_____

One thing we'll always remember about this trip was:

_____

_____

If we visited here again, we would be sure to:

_____

_____

Favorite Memories

_____

_____

_____

_____

Favorite Food: (Best camping recipe, favorite ice cream shop, etc.)

_____

_____

_____

_____

_____

_____

_____

Notes:

_____

_____

_____

_____

_____

_____

_____

Favorite Photo:

Campground: Dates:

We Stayed At Site#: _____   Other Sites We Liked: _____

Location: _____

Weather:

Overall, This Campground Was:

☐ Amazing   ☐ Great   ☐ Fun   ☐ Okay

We camped with:

_____
_____
_____

Our favorite thing to do at this campground was:

_____
_____
_____

One thing we'll always remember about this trip was:

_____
_____
_____

If we visited here again, we would be sure to:

_____
_____

Favorite Memories

_____
_____
_____
_____
_____

Favorite Food: (Best camping recipe, favorite ice cream shop, etc.)

_____

_____

_____

_____

_____

_____

_____

_____

Notes:

_____

_____

_____

_____

_____

_____

_____

_____

Favorite Photo:

Campground: _____   Dates: _____

We Stayed At Site#: _____   Other Sites We Liked: _____

Location: _____

Weather:

Overall, This Campground Was:

☐ Amazing   ☐ Great   ☐ Fun   ☐ Okay

We camped with:

_____
_____
_____

Our favorite thing to do at this campground was:

_____
_____
_____

One thing we'll always remember about this trip was:

_____
_____
_____

If we visited here again, we would be sure to:

_____
_____

Favorite Memories

_____
_____
_____
_____
_____

Favorite Food: (Best camping recipe, favorite ice cream shop, etc.)

_____

_____

_____

_____

_____

_____

_____

Notes:

_____

_____

_____

_____

_____

_____

_____

Favorite Photo:

Campground: _____   Dates: _____

We Stayed At Site#: _____   Other Sites We Liked: _____

Location: _____

Weather: ☀ ☁ 🌧 🌨

Overall, This Campground Was:

☐ Amazing   ☐ Great   ☐ Fun   ☐ Okay

We camped with:

_____
_____
_____

Our favorite thing to do at this campground was:

_____
_____
_____

One thing we'll always remember about this trip was:

_____
_____

If we visited here again, we would be sure to:

_____
_____

Favorite Memories

_____
_____
_____
_____
_____

Favorite Food: (Best camping recipe, favorite ice cream shop, etc.)

_____
_____
_____
_____
_____
_____
_____

Notes:

_____
_____
_____
_____
_____
_____
_____
_____

Favorite Photo:

Campground: _____   **Dates:** _____

We Stayed At Site#: _____   Other Sites We Liked: _____

Location: _____

Weather:

Overall, This Campground Was:

☐ Amazing   ☐ Great   ☐ Fun   ☐ Okay

We camped with:

_____

_____

_____

Our favorite thing to do at this campground was:

_____

_____

_____

One thing we'll always remember about this trip was:

_____

_____

_____

If we visited here again, we would be sure to:

_____

_____

Favorite Memories

_____

_____

_____

_____

_____

Favorite Food: (Best camping recipe, favorite ice cream shop, etc.)

_____
_____
_____
_____
_____
_____
_____

Notes:

_____
_____
_____
_____
_____
_____
_____

Favorite Photo:

Campground: _____ Dates: _____

We Stayed At Site #: _____ Other Sites We Liked: _____

Location: _____

Weather:

Overall, This Campground Was:

☐ Amazing ☐ Great ☐ Fun ☐ Okay

We camped with:

_____
_____
_____

Our favorite thing to do at this campground was:

_____
_____
_____

One thing we'll always remember about this trip was:

_____
_____
_____

If we visited here again, we would be sure to:

_____
_____

Favorite Memories

_____
_____
_____
_____
_____

Favorite Food: (Best camping recipe, favorite ice cream shop, etc.)

_____
_____
_____
_____
_____
_____
_____
_____

Notes:

_____
_____
_____
_____
_____
_____
_____
_____

Favorite Photo:

Campground: _____   **Dates:** _____

We Stayed At Site#: _____   Other Sites We Liked: _____

Location: _____

Weather: ☀ ☁ 🌧 🌨

┌───┐
Overall, This Campground Was:

☐ Amazing   ☐ Great   ☐ Fun   ☐ Okay
└───┘

We camped with:

_____

_____

_____

Our favorite thing to do at this campground was:

_____

_____

_____

One thing we'll always remember about this trip was:

_____

_____

_____

If we visited here again, we would be sure to:

_____

_____

Favorite Memories

_____

_____

_____

_____

_____

Favorite Food: (Best camping recipe, favorite ice cream shop, etc.)

_____
_____
_____
_____
_____
_____
_____
_____

Notes:

_____
_____
_____
_____
_____
_____
_____
_____
_____

Favorite Photo:

Campground: _____ **Dates:** _____

We Stayed At Site#: _____ Other Sites We Liked: _____

Location: _____

Weather: ☀ ☁ 🌧 🌨

Overall, This Campground Was:

☐ Amazing ☐ Great ☐ Fun ☐ Okay

We camped with:

_____
_____
_____

Our favorite thing to do at this campground was:

_____
_____
_____

One thing we'll always remember about this trip was:

_____
_____
_____

If we visited here again, we would be sure to:

_____
_____

Favorite Memories

_____
_____
_____
_____
_____

Favorite Food: (Best camping recipe, favorite ice cream shop, etc.)

_____
_____
_____
_____
_____
_____
_____

Notes:

_____
_____
_____
_____
_____
_____
_____

Favorite Photo:

Campground:	Dates:

We Stayed At Site#: _____   Other Sites We Liked: _____

Location: _____

Weather: ☀ ☁ ⛆ ❄

```
┌─────────────────────────────────────────────┐
│        Overall, This Campground Was:          │
│  ☐ Amazing   ☐ Great   ☐ Fun   ☐ Okay        │
└─────────────────────────────────────────────┘
```

We camped with:

_____
_____
_____

Our favorite thing to do at this campground was:

_____
_____
_____

One thing we'll always remember about this trip was:

_____
_____
_____

If we visited here again, we would be sure to:

_____
_____

Favorite Memories

_____
_____
_____
_____
_____

Favorite Food: (Best camping recipe, favorite ice cream shop, etc.)

_____

_____

_____

_____

_____

_____

_____

Notes:

_____

_____

_____

_____

_____

_____

_____

Favorite Photo:

Campground: _____   Dates: _____

We Stayed At Site#: _____   Other Sites We Liked: _____

Location: _____

Weather: ☀   ☁   🌧   🌨

Overall, This Campground Was:

☐ Amazing   ☐ Great   ☐ Fun   ☐ Okay

We camped with:

_____
_____
_____

Our favorite thing to do at this campground was:

_____
_____
_____

One thing we'll always remember about this trip was:

_____
_____
_____

If we visited here again, we would be sure to:

_____
_____

Favorite Memories

_____
_____
_____
_____
_____

Favorite Food: (Best camping recipe, favorite ice cream shop, etc.)

_____
_____
_____
_____
_____
_____
_____

Notes:

_____
_____
_____
_____
_____
_____
_____
_____

Favorite Photo:

Campground: _____ **Dates:** _____

We Stayed At Site#: _____ Other Sites We Liked: _____

Location: _____

Weather: ☀ ☁ 🌧 🌨

Overall, This Campground Was:
☐ Amazing ☐ Great ☐ Fun ☐ Okay

We camped with:

_____

_____

_____

Our favorite thing to do at this campground was:

_____

_____

_____

One thing we'll always remember about this trip was:

_____

_____

_____

If we visited here again, we would be sure to:

_____

_____

Favorite Memories

_____

_____

_____

_____

_____

Favorite Food: (Best camping recipe, favorite ice cream shop, etc.)

_____
_____
_____
_____
_____
_____
_____
_____

Notes:

_____
_____
_____
_____
_____
_____
_____
_____

Favorite Photo:

Campground: _____   **Dates:** _____

We Stayed At Site#: _____   Other Sites We Liked: _____

Location: _____

Weather:

Overall, This Campground Was:

☐ Amazing   ☐ Great   ☐ Fun   ☐ Okay

We camped with:

_____

_____

_____

Our favorite thing to do at this campground was:

_____

_____

_____

One thing we'll always remember about this trip was:

_____

_____

_____

If we visited here again, we would be sure to:

_____

_____

Favorite Memories

_____

_____

_____

_____

_____

Favorite Food: (Best camping recipe, favorite ice cream shop, etc.)

_____
_____
_____
_____
_____
_____
_____

Notes:

_____
_____
_____
_____
_____
_____
_____
_____

Favorite Photo:

Campground: _____   Dates: _____

We Stayed At Site#: _____   Other Sites We Liked: _____

Location: _____

Weather: ☀ ☁ 🌧 🌨

Overall, This Campground Was:

☐ Amazing   ☐ Great   ☐ Fun   ☐ Okay

We camped with:

_____
_____
_____

Our favorite thing to do at this campground was:

_____
_____
_____

One thing we'll always remember about this trip was:

_____
_____
_____

If we visited here again, we would be sure to:

_____
_____

Favorite Memories

_____
_____
_____
_____
_____

Favorite Food: (Best camping recipe, favorite ice cream shop, etc.)

_____

_____

_____

_____

_____

_____

_____

Notes:

_____

_____

_____

_____

_____

_____

_____

Favorite Photo:

Campground: _____ Dates: _____

We Stayed At Site#: _____ Other Sites We Liked: _____

Location: _____

Weather: ☀ ☁ 🌧 🌨

Overall, This Campground Was:
☐ Amazing ☐ Great ☐ Fun ☐ Okay

We camped with:

_____
_____
_____

Our favorite thing to do at this campground was:

_____
_____
_____

One thing we'll always remember about this trip was:

_____
_____
_____

If we visited here again, we would be sure to:

_____
_____

Favorite Memories

_____
_____
_____
_____
_____

Favorite Food: (Best camping recipe, favorite ice cream shop, etc.)

_____
_____
_____
_____
_____
_____
_____

Notes:

_____
_____
_____
_____
_____
_____

Favorite Photo:

Campground: Dates:

We Stayed At Site#: _____   Other Sites We Liked: _____

Location: _____

Weather: ☀ ☁ 🌧 🌨

Overall, This Campground Was:

☐ Amazing   ☐ Great   ☐ Fun   ☐ Okay

We camped with:

_____
_____
_____

Our favorite thing to do at this campground was:

_____
_____
_____

One thing we'll always remember about this trip was:

_____
_____
_____

If we visited here again, we would be sure to:

_____
_____

Favorite Memories

_____
_____
_____
_____
_____

Favorite Food: (Best camping recipe, favorite ice cream shop, etc.)

_____

_____

_____

_____

_____

_____

_____

Notes:

_____

_____

_____

_____

_____

_____

_____

_____

Favorite Photo:

Campground: _____   Dates: _____

We Stayed At Site#: _____   Other Sites We Liked: _____

Location: _____

Weather:

Overall, This Campground Was:

☐ Amazing   ☐ Great   ☐ Fun   ☐ Okay

We camped with:

_____

_____

_____

Our favorite thing to do at this campground was:

_____

_____

_____

One thing we'll always remember about this trip was:

_____

_____

_____

If we visited here again, we would be sure to:

_____

_____

Favorite Memories

_____

_____

_____

_____

Favorite Food: (Best camping recipe, favorite ice cream shop, etc.)

_____
_____
_____
_____
_____
_____
_____

Notes:

_____
_____
_____
_____
_____
_____
_____

Favorite Photo:

Campground: _____ **Dates:** _____

We Stayed At Site#: _____ Other Sites We Liked: _____

Location: _____

Weather:

Overall, This Campground Was:
☐ Amazing ☐ Great ☐ Fun ☐ Okay

We camped with:

_____
_____
_____

Our favorite thing to do at this campground was:

_____
_____
_____

One thing we'll always remember about this trip was:

_____
_____
_____

If we visited here again, we would be sure to:

_____
_____

Favorite Memories

_____
_____
_____
_____
_____

Favorite Food: (Best camping recipe, favorite ice cream shop, etc.)

_____

_____

_____

_____

_____

_____

_____

Notes:

_____

_____

_____

_____

_____

_____

_____

Favorite Photo:

Campground: Dates:

We Stayed At Site#: _____   Other Sites We Liked: _____

Location: _____

Weather: ☀ 🌧 🌧 🌨

Overall, This Campground Was:

☐ Amazing   ☐ Great   ☐ Fun   ☐ Okay

We camped with:

_____
_____
_____

Our favorite thing to do at this campground was:

_____
_____
_____

One thing we'll always remember about this trip was:

_____
_____
_____

If we visited here again, we would be sure to:

_____
_____

Favorite Memories

_____
_____
_____
_____

Favorite Food: (Best camping recipe, favorite ice cream shop, etc.)

_____
_____
_____
_____
_____
_____
_____

Notes:

_____
_____
_____
_____
_____
_____
_____
_____

Favorite Photo:

Campground: _____ **Dates:** _____

We Stayed At Site#: _____ Other Sites We Liked: _____

Location: _____

Weather:

Overall, This Campground Was:

☐ Amazing ☐ Great ☐ Fun ☐ Okay

We camped with:

_____
_____
_____

Our favorite thing to do at this campground was:

_____
_____
_____

One thing we'll always remember about this trip was:

_____
_____
_____

If we visited here again, we would be sure to:

_____
_____

Favorite Memories

_____
_____
_____
_____

Favorite Food: (Best camping recipe, favorite ice cream shop, etc.)

_____

_____

_____

_____

_____

_____

_____

Notes:

_____

_____

_____

_____

_____

_____

_____

_____

Favorite Photo:

Campground: _____ Dates: _____

We Stayed At Site#: _____ Other Sites We Liked: _____

Location: _____

Weather:

Overall, This Campground Was:

☐ Amazing ☐ Great ☐ Fun ☐ Okay

We camped with:

_____
_____
_____

Our favorite thing to do at this campground was:

_____
_____
_____

One thing we'll always remember about this trip was:

_____
_____
_____

If we visited here again, we would be sure to:

_____
_____

Favorite Memories

_____
_____
_____
_____

Favorite Food: (Best camping recipe, favorite ice cream shop, etc.)

_____

_____

_____

_____

_____

_____

_____

Notes:

_____

_____

_____

_____

_____

_____

_____

_____

Favorite Photo:

Campground: _____   **Dates:** _____

We Stayed At Site#: _____   Other Sites We Liked: _____

Location: _____

Weather:

Overall, This Campground Was:

☐ Amazing   ☐ Great   ☐ Fun   ☐ Okay

We camped with:

_____
_____
_____

Our favorite thing to do at this campground was:

_____
_____
_____

One thing we'll always remember about this trip was:

_____
_____
_____

If we visited here again, we would be sure to:

_____
_____

Favorite Memories

_____
_____
_____
_____

Favorite Food: (Best camping recipe, favorite ice cream shop, etc.)

_____

_____

_____

_____

_____

_____

_____

Notes:

_____

_____

_____

_____

_____

_____

_____

Favorite Photo:

Campground: _____ Dates: _____

We Stayed At Site#: _____ Other Sites We Liked: _____

Location: _____

Weather:

Overall, This Campground Was:

☐ Amazing ☐ Great ☐ Fun ☐ Okay

We camped with:

_____
_____
_____

Our favorite thing to do at this campground was:

_____
_____
_____

One thing we'll always remember about this trip was:

_____
_____
_____

If we visited here again, we would be sure to:

_____
_____

Favorite Memories

_____
_____
_____
_____

Favorite Food: (Best camping recipe, favorite ice cream shop, etc.)

_____
_____
_____
_____
_____
_____
_____

Notes:

_____
_____
_____
_____
_____
_____
_____

Favorite Photo:

Campground: Dates:

We Stayed At Site#: _____   Other Sites We Liked: _____

Location: _____

Weather: Overall, This Campground Was:

☐ Amazing   ☐ Great   ☐ Fun   ☐ Okay

We camped with:

_____
_____
_____

Our favorite thing to do at this campground was:

_____
_____
_____

One thing we'll always remember about this trip was:

_____
_____
_____

If we visited here again, we would be sure to:

_____
_____

Favorite Memories

_____
_____
_____
_____

Favorite Food: (Best camping recipe, favorite ice cream shop, etc.)

_____

_____

_____

_____

_____

_____

_____

Notes:

_____

_____

_____

_____

_____

_____

_____

_____

Favorite Photo:

Campground: _____   Dates: _____

We Stayed At Site#: _____   Other Sites We Liked: _____

Location: _____

Weather:

Overall, This Campground Was:

☐ Amazing   ☐ Great   ☐ Fun   ☐ Okay

We camped with:

_____
_____
_____

Our favorite thing to do at this campground was:

_____
_____
_____

One thing we'll always remember about this trip was:

_____
_____
_____

If we visited here again, we would be sure to:

_____
_____

Favorite Memories

_____
_____
_____
_____

Favorite Food: (Best camping recipe, favorite ice cream shop, etc.)

_____
_____
_____
_____
_____
_____
_____

Notes:

_____
_____
_____
_____
_____
_____
_____

Favorite Photo:

Campground: _____   **Dates:** _____

We Stayed At Site#: _____   Other Sites We Liked: _____

Location: _____

Weather: ☀ ☁ 🌧 🌨

┌───┐
│ Overall, This Campground Was: │
│ ☐ Amazing   ☐ Great   ☐ Fun   ☐ Okay   │
└───┘

We camped with:

_____

_____

_____

Our favorite thing to do at this campground was:

_____

_____

_____

One thing we'll always remember about this trip was:

_____

_____

_____

If we visited here again, we would be sure to:

_____

_____

Favorite Memories

_____

_____

_____

_____

_____

Favorite Food: (Best camping recipe, favorite ice cream shop, etc.)

_____
_____
_____
_____
_____
_____
_____
_____

Notes:

_____
_____
_____
_____
_____
_____
_____
_____

Favorite Photo:

Campground: _____ Dates: _____

We Stayed At Site#: _____ Other Sites We Liked: _____

Location: _____

Weather: ☀ ☁ 🌧 ❄

Overall, This Campground Was:

☐ Amazing ☐ Great ☐ Fun ☐ Okay

We camped with:

_____
_____
_____

Our favorite thing to do at this campground was:

_____
_____
_____

One thing we'll always remember about this trip was:

_____
_____
_____

If we visited here again, we would be sure to:

_____
_____

Favorite Memories

_____
_____
_____
_____

Favorite Food: (Best camping recipe, favorite ice cream shop, etc.)

_____

_____

_____

_____

_____

_____

_____

Notes:

_____

_____

_____

_____

_____

_____

_____

Favorite Photo:

Campground: Dates:

We Stayed At Site#: _____   Other Sites We Liked: _____

Location: _____

Weather: **Overall, This Campground Was:**

☐ Amazing   ☐ Great   ☐ Fun   ☐ Okay

We camped with:

_____
_____
_____

Our favorite thing to do at this campground was:

_____
_____
_____

One thing we'll always remember about this trip was:

_____
_____
_____

If we visited here again, we would be sure to:

_____
_____

Favorite Memories

_____
_____
_____
_____
_____

Favorite Food: (Best camping recipe, favorite ice cream shop, etc.)

_____

_____

_____

_____

_____

_____

_____

Notes:

_____

_____

_____

_____

_____

_____

_____

Favorite Photo:

Campground: _____   **Dates:** _____

We Stayed At Site#: _____   Other Sites We Liked: _____

Location: _____

Weather: ☀ 🌧 🌧 🌨

Overall, This Campground Was:

☐ Amazing   ☐ Great   ☐ Fun   ☐ Okay

We camped with:

_____
_____
_____

Our favorite thing to do at this campground was:

_____
_____
_____

One thing we'll always remember about this trip was:

_____
_____
_____

If we visited here again, we would be sure to:

_____
_____

Favorite Memories

_____
_____
_____
_____

Favorite Food: (Best camping recipe, favorite ice cream shop, etc.)

_____

_____

_____

_____

_____

_____

_____

_____

Notes:

_____

_____

_____

_____

_____

_____

_____

_____

Favorite Photo:

Campground:	Dates:

We Stayed At Site#: _____ Other Sites We Liked: _____

Location: _____

Weather:

Overall, This Campground Was:

☐ Amazing   ☐ Great   ☐ Fun   ☐ Okay

We camped with:

_____
_____
_____

Our favorite thing to do at this campground was:

_____
_____
_____

One thing we'll always remember about this trip was:

_____
_____
_____

If we visited here again, we would be sure to:

_____
_____

Favorite Memories

_____
_____
_____
_____
_____

Favorite Food: (Best camping recipe, favorite ice cream shop, etc.)

_____

_____

_____

_____

_____

_____

_____

Notes:

_____

_____

_____

_____

_____

_____

_____

_____

Favorite Photo:

Campground: _____   **Dates:** _____

We Stayed At Site#: _____   Other Sites We Liked: _____

Location: _____

Weather: ☀ ☁ 🌧 🌨

Overall, This Campground Was:

☐ Amazing   ☐ Great   ☐ Fun   ☐ Okay

We camped with:

_____
_____
_____

Our favorite thing to do at this campground was:

_____
_____
_____

One thing we'll always remember about this trip was:

_____
_____
_____

If we visited here again, we would be sure to:

_____
_____

Favorite Memories

_____
_____
_____
_____

Favorite Food: (Best camping recipe, favorite ice cream shop, etc.)

_____

_____

_____

_____

_____

_____

_____

Notes:

_____

_____

_____

_____

_____

_____

Favorite Photo:

Campground: _____   **Dates:** _____

We Stayed At Site#: _____   Other Sites We Liked: _____

Location: _____

Weather: ☀   ☁   🌧   🌨

Overall, This Campground Was:

☐ Amazing   ☐ Great   ☐ Fun   ☐ Okay

We camped with:

_____
_____
_____

Our favorite thing to do at this campground was:

_____
_____
_____

One thing we'll always remember about this trip was:

_____
_____
_____

If we visited here again, we would be sure to:

_____
_____

Favorite Memories

_____
_____
_____
_____

Favorite Food: (Best camping recipe, favorite ice cream shop, etc.)

_____
_____
_____
_____
_____
_____
_____

Notes:

_____
_____
_____
_____
_____
_____
_____
_____

Favorite Photo:

Campground: Dates:

We Stayed At Site#: _____   Other Sites We Liked: _____

Location: _____

Weather: ☀ ☁ 🌧 🌨

Overall, This Campground Was:

☐ Amazing   ☐ Great   ☐ Fun   ☐ Okay

We camped with:

_____
_____
_____

Our favorite thing to do at this campground was:

_____
_____
_____

One thing we'll always remember about this trip was:

_____
_____
_____

If we visited here again, we would be sure to:

_____
_____

Favorite Memories

_____
_____
_____
_____
_____

Favorite Food: (Best camping recipe, favorite ice cream shop, etc.)

_____
_____
_____
_____
_____
_____
_____

Notes:

_____
_____
_____
_____
_____
_____
_____

Favorite Photo:

Campground: _____ **Dates:** _____

We Stayed At Site#: _____ Other Sites We Liked: _____

Location: _____

Weather:

Overall, This Campground Was:

☐ Amazing   ☐ Great   ☐ Fun   ☐ Okay

We camped with:

_____
_____
_____

Our favorite thing to do at this campground was:

_____
_____
_____

One thing we'll always remember about this trip was:

_____
_____
_____

If we visited here again, we would be sure to:

_____
_____

Favorite Memories

_____
_____
_____
_____
_____

Favorite Food: (Best camping recipe, favorite ice cream shop, etc.)

_____

_____

_____

_____

_____

_____

_____

Notes:

_____

_____

_____

_____

_____

_____

_____

Favorite Photo:

Campground: _____   **Dates:** _____

We Stayed At Site#: _____   Other Sites We Liked: _____

Location: _____

Weather: ☀ 🌥 ⛈ 🌨

Overall, This Campground Was:

☐ Amazing   ☐ Great   ☐ Fun   ☐ Okay

We camped with:

_____

_____

_____

Our favorite thing to do at this campground was:

_____

_____

_____

One thing we'll always remember about this trip was:

_____

_____

_____

If we visited here again, we would be sure to:

_____

_____

Favorite Memories

_____

_____

_____

_____

Favorite Food: (Best camping recipe, favorite ice cream shop, etc.)

_____
_____
_____
_____
_____
_____
_____

Notes:

_____
_____
_____
_____
_____
_____
_____
_____

Favorite Photo:

Campground: _____   Dates: _____

We Stayed At Site#: _____   Other Sites We Liked: _____

Location: _____

Weather: ☀ ☁ 🌧 🌨

Overall, This Campground Was:

☐ Amazing   ☐ Great   ☐ Fun   ☐ Okay

We camped with:

_____
_____
_____

Our favorite thing to do at this campground was:

_____
_____
_____

One thing we'll always remember about this trip was:

_____
_____
_____

If we visited here again, we would be sure to:

_____
_____

Favorite Memories

_____
_____
_____
_____

Favorite Food: (Best camping recipe, favorite ice cream shop, etc.)

_____

_____

_____

_____

_____

_____

_____

Notes:

_____

_____

_____

_____

_____

_____

_____

Favorite Photo:

Campground: _____ **Dates:** _____

We Stayed At Site#: _____ Other Sites We Liked: _____

Location: _____

Weather: ☀ ☁ 🌧 🌩

Overall, This Campground Was:

☐ Amazing ☐ Great ☐ Fun ☐ Okay

We camped with:

_____
_____
_____

Our favorite thing to do at this campground was:

_____
_____
_____

One thing we'll always remember about this trip was:

_____
_____
_____

If we visited here again, we would be sure to:

_____
_____

Favorite Memories

_____
_____
_____
_____

Favorite Food: (Best camping recipe, favorite ice cream shop, etc.)

_____

_____

_____

_____

_____

_____

_____

Notes:

_____

_____

_____

_____

_____

_____

_____

_____

Favorite Photo:

Campground: Dates:

We Stayed At Site#: _____ Other Sites We Liked: _____

Location: _____

Weather: ☀ ☁ 🌧 🌨

┌───┐
│   Overall, This Campground Was: │
│ ☐ Amazing   ☐ Great   ☐ Fun   ☐ Okay   │
└───┘

We camped with:

_____
_____
_____

Our favorite thing to do at this campground was:

_____
_____
_____

One thing we'll always remember about this trip was:

_____
_____
_____

If we visited here again, we would be sure to:

_____
_____

Favorite Memories

_____
_____
_____
_____

Favorite Food: (Best camping recipe, favorite ice cream shop, etc.)

_____

_____

_____

_____

_____

_____

_____

Notes:

_____

_____

_____

_____

_____

_____

_____

_____

Favorite Photo:

Campground:

Dates:

We Stayed At Site#: _____   Other Sites We Liked: _____

Location: _____

Weather: ☀   ☁   🌧   🌨

┌───┐
Overall, This Campground Was:

☐ Amazing   ☐ Great   ☐ Fun   ☐ Okay
└───┘

We camped with:

_____

_____

_____

Our favorite thing to do at this campground was:

_____

_____

_____

One thing we'll always remember about this trip was:

_____

_____

_____

If we visited here again, we would be sure to:

_____

_____

Favorite Memories

_____

_____

_____

_____

Favorite Food: (Best camping recipe, favorite ice cream shop, etc.)

_____

_____

_____

_____

_____

_____

_____

Notes:

_____

_____

_____

_____

_____

_____

_____

Favorite Photo:

Campground: _____ Dates: _____

We Stayed At Site#: _____ Other Sites We Liked: _____

Location: _____

Weather:

Overall, This Campground Was:

☐ Amazing ☐ Great ☐ Fun ☐ Okay

We camped with:

_____
_____
_____

Our favorite thing to do at this campground was:

_____
_____
_____

One thing we'll always remember about this trip was:

_____
_____
_____

If we visited here again, we would be sure to:

_____
_____

Favorite Memories

_____
_____
_____
_____

Favorite Food: (Best camping recipe, favorite ice cream shop, etc.)

_____
_____
_____
_____
_____
_____
_____

Notes:

_____
_____
_____
_____
_____
_____
_____
_____

Favorite Photo:

Campground: _____   Dates: _____

We Stayed At Site#: _____   Other Sites We Liked: _____

Location: _____

Weather:

Overall, This Campground Was:

☐ Amazing   ☐ Great   ☐ Fun   ☐ Okay

We camped with:

_____

_____

_____

Our favorite thing to do at this campground was:

_____

_____

_____

One thing we'll always remember about this trip was:

_____

_____

_____

If we visited here again, we would be sure to:

_____

_____

Favorite Memories

_____

_____

_____

_____

Favorite Food: (Best camping recipe, favorite ice cream shop, etc.)

_____

_____

_____

_____

_____

_____

_____

Notes:

_____

_____

_____

_____

_____

_____

_____

Favorite Photo:

Campground: _____ **Dates:** _____

We Stayed At Site#: _____   Other Sites We Liked: _____

Location: _____

Weather:

Overall, This Campground Was:

☐ Amazing   ☐ Great   ☐ Fun   ☐ Okay

We camped with:

_____
_____
_____

Our favorite thing to do at this campground was:

_____
_____
_____

One thing we'll always remember about this trip was:

_____
_____
_____

If we visited here again, we would be sure to:

_____
_____

Favorite Memories

_____
_____
_____
_____

Favorite Food: (Best camping recipe, favorite ice cream shop, etc.)

_____

_____

_____

_____

_____

_____

_____

Notes:

_____

_____

_____

_____

_____

_____

_____

Favorite Photo:

Campground: _____ **Dates:** _____

We Stayed At Site#: _____ Other Sites We Liked: _____

Location: _____

Weather: ☀ ☁ 🌧 🌨

Overall, This Campground Was:

☐ Amazing ☐ Great ☐ Fun ☐ Okay

We camped with:

_____
_____
_____

Our favorite thing to do at this campground was:

_____
_____
_____

One thing we'll always remember about this trip was:

_____
_____
_____

If we visited here again, we would be sure to:

_____
_____

Favorite Memories

_____
_____
_____
_____
_____

Favorite Food: (Best camping recipe, favorite ice cream shop, etc.)

_____
_____
_____
_____
_____
_____
_____

Notes:

_____
_____
_____
_____
_____
_____
_____
_____

Favorite Photo:

Campground: Dates:

We Stayed At Site#: _____   Other Sites We Liked: _____

Location: _____

Weather:

Overall, This Campground Was:

☐ Amazing   ☐ Great   ☐ Fun   ☐ Okay

We camped with:

_____
_____
_____

Our favorite thing to do at this campground was:

_____
_____
_____

One thing we'll always remember about this trip was:

_____
_____
_____

If we visited here again, we would be sure to:

_____
_____

Favorite Memories

_____
_____
_____
_____
_____

Favorite Food: (Best camping recipe, favorite ice cream shop, etc.)

_____
_____
_____
_____
_____
_____
_____

Notes:

_____
_____
_____
_____
_____
_____
_____

Favorite Photo:

Campground: _____   Dates: _____

We Stayed At Site#: _____   Other Sites We Liked: _____

Location: _____

Weather:

Overall, This Campground Was:

☐ Amazing   ☐ Great   ☐ Fun   ☐ Okay

We camped with:

_____
_____
_____

Our favorite thing to do at this campground was:

_____
_____
_____

One thing we'll always remember about this trip was:

_____
_____
_____

If we visited here again, we would be sure to:

_____
_____

Favorite Memories

_____
_____
_____
_____

Favorite Food: (Best camping recipe, favorite ice cream shop, etc.)

_____

_____

_____

_____

_____

_____

_____

Notes:

_____

_____

_____

_____

_____

_____

_____

Favorite Photo:

Printed in Great Britain
by Amazon